PENGUIN BOOKS

BURNING AMBITION

What the media say about the Allen Carr method:

'A different approach. A stunning success.'   *Sun*

'Allen Carr explodes the myth that giving up smoking is difficult.'   *The Times*

'I was exhilarated by a new sense of freedom.'
Independent

'An intelligent and original method.'
Evening Standard

What doctors and other experts say about the Allen Carr method:

'I have no hesitation in supporting Allen Carr's work in helping smokers quit. Many quitting clinics use some of his techniques, but it would appear few do so in quite such a successful package.'
*A personal view from Professor
Judith Mackay, MBE, Director, Asian Consultancy
on Tobacco Control and World Health Organization
Expert, Advisory Panel on Tobacco and Health*

'It is a remarkable fact that Allen Carr [...] should have succeeded where countless psychologists and psychiatrists [...] have failed, in formulating a SIMPLE and EFFECTIVE way to stop smoking.'

Dr William Green, Head of the Psychiatric Department, Matilda Hospital, Hong Kong

'I was really impressed by the method. In spite of Allen Carr's success and fame, there were no gimmicks and the professional approach was something a GP could readily expect. I would be happy to give a medical endorsement of the method to anyone.'
Dr P. M. Bray

'I have observed the Allen Carr method, "The Easy-way to Stop Smoking", at first hand on several occasions. I have found it to be very successful. I wholeheartedly support it as an effective way to stop smoking.'

Dr Anil Visram, B.Sc., MBBch, FRCA, Consultant, The Royal Hospitals NHS Trust, Royal London Hospital, UK

Celebrity endorsements of the Allen Carr method:

'His method is absolutely unique, removing the dependence on cigarettes, while you are actually smoking. I'm pleased to say it has worked for many of my friends and my staff.' *Sir Richard Branson*

'Some friends of mine who had stopped smoking using Allen Carr's method suggested that I try it. I did. It was such a revelation that instantly I was freed from my addiction. Like those friends of mine, I found it not only easy but unbelievably enjoyable to stay stopped.' *Sir Anthony Hopkins*

'For the past 20 years or so, I've been sending clients wishing to stop smoking to the clinics run by Britain's internationally renowned quit-smoking expert, Allen Carr. Allen has a remarkably high success rate at his worldwide network of clinics . . . I believe it's a public health scandal that the taxpayer-funded quit-smoking authorities in this and other countries don't seek Allen's advice and guidance as many major international companies do.' *Carole Caplin*

'A friend of mine went to see a therapist and stopped easily . . . then three more friends went, they experienced no weight gain and no withdrawal symptoms. After seven of my friends had been and stopped smoking easily, I couldn't ignore it any more. The time I spent with Allen Carr was some of the most important and effective since I smoked that first cigarette when I was fourteen. If it didn't sound so embarrassing I'd tell you it changed my life. It's really easy. It really, really works and you don't put on weight.'
Emma Freud

'I stopped with an Allen Carr's Easyway to Stop Smoking Seminar. I wanted to feel free, not a slave to nicotine which does not give you any pleasure.'
Gianluca Vialli

'I stopped smoking . . . I read this book by Allen Carr. It's called the *Easy Way to Stop Smoking*. Everyone who reads this book stops smoking!'
Ellen DeGeneres

Burning Ambition

The Inspiring Story of
One Man's Quest to Cure
the World of Smoking

Allen Carr

PENGUIN BOOKS

PENGUIN BOOKS

Published by the Penguin Group
Penguin Books Ltd, 80 Strand, London WC2R 0RL, England
Penguin Group (USA) Inc., 375 Hudson Street, New York, New York 10014, USA
Penguin Group (Canada), 90 Eglinton Avenue East, Suite 700, Toronto,
Ontario, Canada M4P 2Y3 (a division of Pearson Penguin Canada Inc.)
Penguin Ireland, 25 St Stephen's Green, Dublin 2, Ireland (a division of Penguin Books Ltd)
Penguin Books Australia Ltd, 250 Camberwell Road,
Camberwell, Victoria 3124, Australia (a division of Pearson Australia Group Pty Ltd)
Penguin Books India Pvt Ltd, 11 Community Centre,
Panchsheel Park, New Delhi – 110 017, India
Penguin Group (NZ), 67 Apollo Drive, Rosedale, North Shore 0632, New Zealand
(a division of Pearson New Zealand Ltd)
Penguin Books (South Africa) (Pty) Ltd, 24 Sturdee Avenue,
Rosebank, Johannesburg 2196, South Africa

Penguin Books Ltd, Registered Offices: 80 Strand, London WC2R 0RL, England

www.penguin.com

First published 2007
2

Set in 12/16 pt Stone Serif
Typeset by Rowland Phototypesetting Ltd, Bury St Edmunds, Suffolk
Printed in England by Clays Ltd, St Ives plc

ISBN: 978–0–141–03030–2

To Joyce and Serendipity

Also, special thanks to Tessa Rose,
Nigel Matheson and Hazel Orme for their
patience and perseverance in the
unenviable task of making what
I have written readable

Contents

Publisher's Note

Allen Carr was diagnosed with lung cancer in the summer of 2006 and passed away peacefully in his sleep with Joyce at his bedside on 29 November 2006. Many thought it likely that the years spent in smoke-filled rooms at his clinics played a part in his illnesss. On diagnosis, Allen Carr said, 'I am told that I have cured at least 10 million smokers. If that is the case, it is a price worth paying.' Before his death, he added that, 'Since I smoked my last cigarette, twenty-three years ago, I have been the happiest man in the world and I still feel the same.'

Allen Carr was an ambitious man with an inspiring story to tell, and his methods will carry on helping smokers to quit. As Robin Hayley, Worldwide Managing Director of Allen Carr's Easyway said, 'The fact that a former 100-a-day smoker, having quit in his middle age, lived to the ripe old age of seventy-two is a great message to all smokers. Allen leaves behind an amazing ongoing publishing programme and a worldwide group of clinics that will continue his success.'

Introduction

SOME YEARS AGO I had everything I wanted but something was missing. I had a problem that was killing me. Time after time I had tried to quit smoking and I had always failed.

In the end, luck got me off that hook. I found a way to quit smoking that I called Easyway. I knew it was not just a cure for me. It was a cure for all smokers. If I could beat my 100-a-day habit, then anyone could quit. This led me to take up the quest against smoking.

In this book you can learn about my life. It may remind you of battles you, your family or friends have had with smoking. If so, I hope to be able to show you that there is a way to stop.

I read not long ago that dry-cleaning was invented when a man spilt some paraffin on to a dirty table-cloth. He saw that the bit it had soaked was clean. Was he the first person to spill paraffin on a table-cloth? Perhaps not.

Many had done so before. But he was the first to turn that accident to good use. I did the same with Easyway. This story will tell you how it happened. It is a story of a smoking addiction and how it was overcome, and of a struggle to bring to life something new. That something would change my life and the lives of millions of people.

1 FAMILY LIFE

MY FIRST MEMORY IS of lying, aged two, on my father while he slept in his chair. I felt the rise and fall of his chest and I smelt the beer on his breath. That was as close as I ever got to him.

We lived in Putney, south-west London. At that time it was a working-class area and Dad was a builder. He liked drinking at the local pub, betting on horses, and smoking.

Dad made plenty of money, but he still used a barrow to take his tools to work. He never had a van. I knew him for more than thirty years, and he lived in the same house for twenty. He saw no need to better himself. I did not know him very well, even if he was my dad.

Most kids love their father. I respected mine and was a bit scared of him. The only time he hit me was at one Christmas dinner. He got back late from the pub, drunk, and my mother started to nag him. He wanted to hit her, but I was good at boxing and stopped him. He sprang at me very fast and I was helpless. He put his hands round my throat and there was murder in his eyes. I must have looked scared because he suddenly let go. My mother didn't say a word.

She saw life as hard. She was the eldest of fourteen children. Her mother drank and her father left them. Mum was still a child herself when she became mother and father to her brothers and sisters in the 1930s. Her view of life had a strong effect on me, my older sister Marion and two younger brothers, Derek and John.

When Dad was at home he sat in front of the fire, reading his paper. He had difficulty telling us kids apart because we all had red hair. He knew our names. He knew the order in which we'd been born. But he didn't know which red-haired brat was the cause of any trouble so he told us all off. 'Allen! Derek! John!' Then he had done his duty, and went back to the paper.

Our mother was the main force in the family, but I don't think she talked to us much either. Dad didn't try to talk to us, and Mum didn't know how to. I loved her, and I knew she loved me, but I was the bane of her life. When we boys were fighting, she smacked me. Often I had started the trouble, but she did not bother to ask what it was about before she hit me. I didn't mind being smacked when I knew I had done wrong, but I did mind when someone else had!

However, Mum and Dad gave me the best gift ever. My life. The smacks, with everything else they did, helped me to learn not to take anything for granted. It was an important lesson, but I learnt it the hard way.

2 MAKING THE GRADE

I WAS A STREET child, like all my friends. At each school I went to, the teachers told me, just as my mother had, that I was naughty. I learnt to read, write and count, but that was about it. Then, when I was ten, I had to take an exam. It was called the eleven-plus. The teachers said it was important, but I was sure I would fail so I didn't worry about it.

Then something funny happened: I passed, and was given a place at a good local school. They never said so, but I think my parents were as shocked as I was.

My joy at being chosen to go to that school soon left me when I heard that lots of other children who lived near my house were going too. When the war ended, a new law meant that every child had an equal chance in education. However, at these good schools, each year was split into three. The A form was for boys from well-off families. The C form was for street kids. The B form, in the middle, was a mixture of street kids too clever for the C form, and well-off kids too thick for the A form. I joined the B form.

Boys went up a form or stayed put, depending on how well they did in the summer exams. Luck, rather than hard work, took me from B to A. Lots of boys from the A and C forms left the school in year four, so the numbers in the three forms were uneven. My teachers agreed that I should move to the A form.

I have no doubt that this event was one of the most important in my life. In the B form I was a king, and proud to be a tearaway. I'd even been to court for stealing from an army warehouse, and was heading for a life of petty crime.

But I found school boring, until I got to my last year. I wanted to find a well-paid job and for that I had to pass my O levels, as GCSEs were called. I worked hard and did well in maths, French, geography, history and English. Before we sat those exams, people came to school to talk to us about work in accounting and law. We were led towards work in offices, not on building sites or in factories.

I didn't like my teachers much and I didn't like Mr Smith at all. He tried to make you look small in front of your friends. I had little to do with him until I was sent to him for careers advice. He said: 'You are good at maths. You should go into accounting.' I had no idea what that meant, but I took him at his word and went into a career that I hated.

My marks in my O-level exams were high enough to get me into accounting, but not high enough for university, even if I had wanted to go. Anyway, Mum and Dad told me that the headmaster said I wasn't clever enough. Many years later, my mother said that in fact my marks had been high enough but she and Dad could not afford it. She thought they had acted for the best. And perhaps they had. After all, if my life had been different, I might not have set up Easyway and helped so many people to stop smoking.

When I left school I was still a non-smoker. In fact, I hadn't smoked a cigarette since I was ten, when I had shared a packet of five

Woodbines with two other boys. I had felt sick, but told my mates that the cigarette was very nice. The truth was, I had hated it.

3 THE REAL WORLD

I WAS LUCKY TO be taken on by a big accounting firm with branches all over the world. At fifteen I was an office boy, making tea, running errands and sticking stamps on envelopes. I did this ten times faster than anyone else. Although I did not like the work, and I was not being trained in accounting, it was worth while. The office was well run, and I did the tasks I was told to do.

After a year, I saw that the firm would be happy for me to lick stamps and boots for ever. I told my boss I was going to leave unless I got some training. I wanted to qualify as an accountant. The firm agreed to move me to another department.

It was there that I began to smoke. Trying that Woodbine should have kept me free for life, but I didn't understand the power of nicotine. I was put to work with a smoker called

Ron. Every time Ron lit up, he offered me a cigarette and I reminded him that I didn't smoke. Now, Ron was sharp, but he always forgot that I didn't smoke. I don't think he meant to get me hooked. Perhaps he was just being polite. Anyway, I gave in. I sensed that Ron needed a fellow smoker. And the more cigarettes he gave me, the less I felt sick. Soon I was taking every one he offered.

One morning, as he gave me the first of the day, he joked, 'You keep smoking my cigarettes! When are you going to buy some?'

'Buy some? Who'd pay good money for those filthy things? I told you I didn't smoke, but you kept pushing them at me. I was doing you a favour!' That was what I wanted to say but, of course, I didn't. For many years I believed that I kept my mouth shut so that I didn't upset him.

Ron's words made me buy my first packet, and from then on I offered him as many as he offered me. The idea that my actions were shaped, first, by a wish to help someone out and, second, to avoid hurting their feelings was the kind of lie that most smokers tell themselves. I could have offered Ron a cigarette now

11

and then without smoking one myself. But I was stuck in the smoking trap, smoking a lot and thinking I needed cigarettes to help me focus on my work. That was bad, but I didn't know then that my new habit was about to cost me every spare penny I had.

Like most boys at that time, I was forced to join the army, the navy or the RAF. However, I saw it as an escape from the nightmare I was living at my accounting job. I was excited at the thought of spending two years away from it. But the camp at RAF Padgate was a gloomy place and we often went hungry.

When I was there, I spent some of my savings on chocolate bars in the canteen, and Mum kept me alive by sending me food parcels. Every Friday we were given our wages and by Tuesday we were broke. I had started smoking roll-ups before I went into the forces. They were cheap. I had planned to quit smoking when I joined up, but the first weeks were hard and I put it off. Soon my savings had all gone on tobacco as well as chocolate.

After Padgate I was sent in 1952 to an army camp near Wolverhampton, where I learnt how to load, fire, clean and strip a rifle as well as how to march in step. When my eight weeks were nearly over, an officer asked me if I wanted to be a drill instructor. It seemed like a joke and I laughed. But he wasn't joking. He said that I had to train for eight weeks at RAF Uxbridge. That sold the idea to me. It was just an hour from my home and my friends.

When I had finished my two years in the forces, I was a different person from the shy boy I had once been. Soon, love was in the air. Ellen Healey worked at a small firm in London's East End. She had long, brown hair and lots of charm. I didn't think she had her eye on me, because she liked to talk about her boyfriend and the problems she had with him. At last I was brave enough to ask her out. Nine months later we got married.

I had put off the evil day of returning to my accounting job for as long as I could and now there were two of us to support. However, working for a firm like that meant that I began to understand money and how to make more of it. I soon learnt that accounts never told the exact truth about profits. Perhaps a firm wanted to avoid tax or let its bank think it was doing better than it was. Soon I could read between the lines. It was a useful skill when, later, I worked out the truth about smoking.

After a year in the City, I started to look for a job I would enjoy and found one with a small company that needed an accountant. I was not sure if I would sink or swim. Soon after I started my new job, I made my next attempt to quit smoking. I changed from cigarettes to a pipe. As any pipe-smoker will tell you, you have to get used to the pipe as well as the horrible smell. Sucking the stem made the tip of my tongue so sore that it felt like it had a boil on it. But the worst part was cleaning out the goo that collects in the bowl.

Three months later my tongue was still sore, and I didn't like the taste of the tobacco. I was smoking two ounces a day, and having 'just one' cigarette now and then. Soon I had given up the pipe and was smoking cigarettes again.

I had tried many times to give up smoking, and now I thought quitting was out of the question. Instead I would try to cut down to ten a day. At first this worked well. Each hour of every day, I had a prize to look forward to. Soon I was watching the clock. I never let myself light up one minute early. Sometimes I would stand there, a cigarette in my mouth, waiting for the hand on the clock to get to the top. It took ten minutes to smoke that cigarette. Then I had to wait fifty for the next.

Then a day came when everything went wrong and I couldn't hold back. No problem, I told myself. I'll start again tomorrow.

The Irish comedian Dave Allen summed up what can happen when you try to control your smoking: 'I have a very strict rule about smoking. I never smoke more than an average of ten cigarettes a day. I might borrow the odd cigarette from the next day's quota, but I never exceed the average of ten a day. The cigarette I am now smoking is part of my quota for the fourth of July 2046!'

I didn't fall into this trap. In fact, I did the opposite. When the first hour was up, I didn't light a cigarette, and went the next hour without one. Sometimes I would smoke only one or two cigarettes all day. I was like a squirrel burying nuts for the winter. But it wasn't helping me to stop smoking or making cigarettes seem less important. The first time I built up ten credits, I was like a child counting money from a piggy-bank. I could smoke twenty cigarettes the next day. Bliss!

But the day after *that* was hell. I had to go back to one cigarette an hour. I could not survive on one cigarette an hour. I tried one every half-hour. Perhaps twenty a day wasn't so bad. In the end I decided not to smoke at all in the daytime and to save the whole lot for when I got home. Again, it was great in the beginning. All day I would not smoke and I would feel like a saint. At five-thirty I would rush home and light up. That first cigarette was fantastic. The next? Not quite as good. By the time I was smoking the fifth, I'd be thinking, 'Why am I doing this?'

My next attempt to give up smoking came after I had spent two years as an accountant. I was ready to move on again when I saw an ad for assistant accountants. I did not want to be an assistant, but the wage was high and the firm was well known. I went for an interview.

The office was in a gloomy building a twenty-minute walk from home. I did not much like the man who would be my boss. I decided that this firm was not for me. Then the man said, 'We do not allow smoking in the office.' Today that is normal, but in the early sixties it was not. You might have thought those words would put me off, but when I was offered the job, I took it.

I'm the only person I know who has taken a job he didn't want just to quit smoking! A few months earlier I had seen my father in hospital. He was dying of lung cancer and he was fifty-six. I thought he didn't know I was there, but he opened his eyes and spoke to me. He made me promise to quit smoking. I'd already decided that no way would I end up like him. The moment I left the hospital, I lit a cigarette.

The offer of that job had given me a chance to keep my promise and to halt my health problems. I could afford the best cigarettes and as many of them as I wanted. The effects of so much smoking were becoming more and more obvious.

For some smokers the biggest problem is the need to smoke when they go out. They can say no to cigarettes when they are working, but in a pub, a restaurant or with friends they must have a cigarette. Other smokers think they can't focus without a cigarette. I was one of those, so if I worked in an office where I wasn't allowed to smoke, I thought I would have to quit. But as I found out years later, forcing yourself to quit never leads to success.

My office hours were nine to five with an hour for lunch. I spent the mornings waiting for lunch and the afternoons waiting for five o'clock. If I had a tricky problem, I would have a crafty cigarette in the toilet to help myself solve it. When I had to do overtime, I needed a cigarette so badly at five o'clock that I just had to get out. I had promised to work late and then had to find an excuse not to do so. My job came second to my need to smoke. After six months I could stand it no longer and looked for another job. I took the first I was offered.

It came from a firm that had been formed to market the 'Autolock'. It was intended to protect cars against theft. I enjoyed the time I spent there. I worked all the hours under the sun to catch up with the backlog. There was no going to the toilets for a smoke. I was kept so busy that it took me a long time to see that the firm was going bust. Soon I was out of a job. After six weeks of panic, I got an interview at a large company, the biggest toymaker in the world. I was offered the job and accepted a cut in salary.

It was time for yet another attempt to quit smoking. So far I had failed because I lacked will-power. Now I hit on a brilliant new plan: I would stop buying cigarettes. I warned friends that I'd accept all offers of cigarettes without feeling I had to pay them back.

Now people who had never offered me a cigarette began to do so. This was typical of drug addiction. When you are hooked and needing a fix, no one will give you one. But once another addict senses you are trying to escape, they will do all they can to keep you in the trap.

However, the supply soon dried up until only one person, my secretary, was keeping me going. Half of me hated her for pushing the drug, but the other half loved her because she was my life-line. After a few weeks I was feeling guilty, but stuck to my plan not to buy cigarettes. Then my brain solved the problem: buy *her* a packet, it said. Soon I was buying three packets of her favourite brand every day. I could now accept her cigarettes without guilt and still kid myself that I was stopping smoking because I did not like her brand. A few weeks later I was buying my favourite brand for myself.

I left that firm when it collapsed, and decided I would never again work for someone else. I had seen at first hand why a business could fail, and thought I could do better than the people I'd been working for. However, to set up my own business, I would need all the help I could get. It came from a most unexpected place.

4 TROUBLES AT HOME

IT IS HARD TO know when my first marriage started to go wrong. I believe the seeds were sown when Ellen was carrying our first son, John. She had blood-pressure problems, which caused her to worry so much that her fears got to me. I was sure I would lose my wife and our baby.

All four pregnancies were the same, but we were blessed with four perfect babies: John, Karen, Suzanne and Richard. I loved Ellen but I found her fears so difficult to cope with that I became depressed. I wanted my home to be free of tension and worry. Instead, it became a place I avoided.

There is a famous Nat King Cole song with the lines, 'I was walking along minding my business, when out of an orange-coloured sky – FLASH! BAM! ALAKAZAM! – wonderful you came by.' One night, before I had decided to work for myself, I was at the office. It was late and I was alone because everyone else had gone home. I heard footsteps in the corridor. I looked up just as a girl walked past my door. She had long legs and a mass of jet-black hair piled on top of her head. Her eyes flashed at me as she passed – 'FLASH! BAM! ALAKAZAM!' It was as if I'd been struck by lightning.

That was my first sight of Joyce, who had a personality to match her looks. She had been taken on as an evening temp to clear a backlog of invoices from Christmas. Soon she had joined the staff, and I asked her out for a drink.

When we knew we were in love, we tried to end it. I was the weak link. After surviving two weeks apart, I told Joyce life wasn't worth living without her. She felt the same. We did not want to end our marriages or hurt our families, but we had to run that risk rather than not see each other.

For some years we played our parts at work and at home. Ellen met Joyce and her husband, Ray, at a work party and the four of us began to go out together as friends, so Joyce and I saw more of each other. I liked Ray, too, and we got on well. When the firm ran into deep trouble, we discussed how we could keep going, and Ray told me of his plan to start a business in damp-proofing. When our firm collapsed, we became partners in our own business.

A few months after we had got started, Ray found out about Joyce and me. I thought he would come after me with an axe, but he wanted us to stay partners. The business was taking off and he did not want to see it fail. He thought and he told me that Joyce had already forgotten about me. In fact, she and I had agreed to part for the sake of our families. I still loved her, and I guessed her feelings for me had not changed.

After a few weeks I stopped pretending that I could spend the rest of my life without her, and went to see her. I had been right about her love for me. I handed the business to Ray, and Joyce and I left the area to start afresh in west London, where my mother and sister lived. I had set up one damp-proofing business and knew I could do it again. Aqua-Damp went well from the start, and we soon expanded into timber treatments. They were as simple to do as damp-proofing and soon I felt confident that

I could do a good job at both. I was as happy as a hippo in mud.

I enjoyed building the business, but there were drawbacks. The more successful we were, the more customers and staff we had and the more problems came with them.

After two years Aqua-Damp had eight branches, and I envied the people we provided our services to. Most were couples who had bought rundown houses to do up and sell on at a profit. It seemed a great way to make a living: no customers, no staff, you could live where you wanted, start and finish work when you liked. I knew about electric wiring and plumbing and was also a dab hand with plaster. We wouldn't need to pay anyone to do the work for us. Then a four-bedroom house in a good area came on the market at a very cheap price.

One morning I was looking for a piece of scrap paper and took a crumpled letter out of the bin. I'm not sure why I read it, but I did: it was an offer to buy my business. I asked Joyce why she hadn't shown it to me. She said that we were doing so well that she knew I wouldn't want to sell up.

I told her of my idea to do up houses. She

didn't want to take the risk. I drove her to see my 'find', hoping to put her mind at rest. It had the opposite effect. I saw that house as it would be after we'd done it up. Joyce saw it as it was – dark and dismal.

But I was sure it wouldn't take much to put it right, and that we could do it if we got a good price for Aqua-Damp, which we did. We spent six months working on the house and Joyce was so happy with the result that she didn't want to sell it.

Doing up houses was a pleasant way to earn a living. Over five years we fixed up ten shabby, run-down houses, and Joyce became an expert at tiling, painting and paper-hanging. They were happy years and we made a good living.

Our new way of life had only two drawbacks. First, Joyce never wanted to move into the next run-down house, and, when it was finished, she never wanted to leave it. I could not shrug off the second drawback so easily.

I was forty-eight and the work was demanding. I had a cough, and often suffered with chest problems. I put it down to my age. I'd had that hacking cough for at least twenty years.

I can still see my father as he was sixty years

ago, cigarette between his lips, dropping ash on the carpet, eyes watering, coughing up his lungs each morning. When I asked him why he smoked, he said he 'enjoyed' it. I couldn't understand that. It was clear to me that he got no pleasure from it.

I knew I did not enjoy smoking. But I did believe that smoking gave me confidence, courage and helped me to focus. I hated being a smoker and had tried hard to quit. But every time I did, I felt naked without a cigarette.

In my latest attempt I had taken the advice of ex-smokers and kept a packet of cigarettes on me to make me feel in control. It didn't work because I needed to smoke those cigarettes. They were no good to me in the packet. When I had a mental task to do, I wanted a cigarette. I had six months of misery, and my need to smoke didn't go away, as many ex-smokers had said it would. Instead it got worse, and I gave in to it rather than giving up. I cried like a baby because I knew I'd never have the will-power to go through that misery again and that I was doomed to be a slave to nicotine for the rest of my life. I was sure I'd always be a smoker because I had a basic flaw in my character. Then, one evening, I was watching television and heard Denis Norden say, 'I woke up and my throat was like a cess-pit. I decided there and then to quit and I'm ashamed to say it was easy. I had no withdrawal pangs, and I've never had the desire to smoke since.'

The next morning I woke with his words on my mind. The idea of it being easy to quit smoking had not occurred to me before. All the ex-smokers I knew had said how hard it was. It was clear that Denis had not had to use will-power to stop smoking. But the main point was that he had not had the urge to smoke since he quit. I had never met an ex-smoker who did not crave a cigarette from time to time. Now I thought about quitting as an escape from addiction, not as a period of misery that had to be endured to 'give up' a crutch and a pleasure.

I decided to try quitting again, this time adopting Denis Norden's frame of mind. It worked. It was so easy that after three weeks I felt free. I said to Joyce, 'I've kicked it! I'll celebrate with a Hamlet!' Three months later I was chain-smoking Hamlets.

After so many attempts to quit I should have

learnt that you can't have 'just one' cigarette. I suppose my mind did not accept that I would never be able to smoke 'just one' cigarette ever again. I believed that smoking was a habit, and that if I had got into it I should be able to get out of it.

My failed attempts to stop smoking upset me. When you live in a house of smokers and fail to quit, the others feel relief. But I lived with Joyce, who had never smoked. The pain of a failed attempt was greater each time. Finally, I could not bring myself to tell Joyce I had failed. I decided not to smoke in her company, or with friends in case they told her.

Of course it was not long before I was smoking again with friends. I asked them not to tell Joyce, and soon everyone except Joyce knew I was smoking. Being a slave to a drug has many evil aspects, but for me this was the worst. I pride myself on being honest, but for cigarettes I could lie to and cheat my wife.

As I lost the battle to limit my intake, things got even worse. I would send Joyce out to buy things I didn't need. The moment I heard the car start, I would light up. I would work out the time of her return and fifteen minutes before she was due I would put out the cigarette and open the windows. Later, I had to hear the car come back before I stubbed out the cigarette. Every time a car went by I rushed to the window to see if it was Joyce.

I had reached the stage where I was prepared to lose someone I loved – and, worse, to hurt her – just so that I could remain an addict. At any excuse, I would march off in a huff. I wasn't really in a huff. I wanted to smoke so I had to get away from her. Once we had set up home together, I stopped going to pubs. But then I began to cause rows so that I could stomp off to the pub and fill my lungs with smoke until closing time.

Finally, Joyce said, 'Are you going to tell me about it?' I blushed, thinking she had found me out. I tried to pretend I did not know what she meant. 'You're carrying on with another woman, aren't you?' she said.

I told her the truth at last. She had no rival for my love, just a rival for my company – nicotine. As much as I hated it, I could not do without it. Joyce was so relieved that I wasn't seeing another woman that the truth was almost a cause for joy.

But, as the effects on me of smoking became harder to ignore, she begged me to keep trying to quit. Sometimes she would tell me how so-and-so had quit using such-and-such a method. I didn't listen to her. She could not understand why a smart, strong-willed man could put himself through the misery of being a smoker. I couldn't understand it either. I knew the pain I was causing her, and that I was weak and selfish for not stopping.

Then came the morning of 15 July 1983. I was on my way to the car when I had a coughing fit, which started a nosebleed. When the bleeding stopped, I felt as low as I had ever been and lit a cigarette. The bleeding started again. Joyce came to find out why I hadn't driven off and found me sitting in the car, blood soaking the burning cigarette in my mouth.

She told me to see a man who had helped a friend of ours to quit. He was a 'hypnotherapist'. I agreed. I knew that smoking would kill me, which made me want to quit, but it didn't help me do it, any more than my father's death had helped.

For me that day had started in misery. It turned out to be the best day of my life.

5 THE GREAT ESCAPE

HAVE YOU EVER USED one of those plastic fillers to plug gaps in wood? You mix the contents of two tubes, and it sets as hard as rock. When I escaped from smoking, two factors combined and set in my mind.

I was not aware of either when I made my way to the hypno-therapist's clinic. He was a bright young man. We had a chat about smoking, and then he said, 'Did you know that smoking is just nicotine addiction and if you quit for long enough you will be free?' I cannot remember anything else he said, but that statement stayed in my brain.

I used to call myself a nicotine addict in the same way that I called myself a golf addict. I thought that nicotine was a nasty substance that stained my teeth and fingers. I had never seen it as a drug like heroin. Smoking was a habit. OK, it was difficult to break, but I did not think of it as drug addiction. I believed that heroin was the great evil, even though it kills fewer than 300 people a year in the UK. Nicotine kills more than 2,000 every week.

Like many smokers I couldn't understand why I smoked. The therapist had explained I was addicted to a drug. Now I saw myself on a par with a heroin addict, not just as a smoker. But the bit that really stuck in my mind was: 'If you quit for long enough you will be free.'

Now that I saw myself in a new light, as someone addicted to a drug, I believed I could quit. I didn't care how long it took. I didn't expect it to be easy. I had about five cigarettes left in the packet and decided that they would be the last I would smoke.

I didn't tell the hypno-therapist how I felt, but the session was now pointless. The moment I left the clinic I lit up then made my way home, the hypno-therapist's words still going round in my head.

John, my elder son, gave me the second piece of information. Joyce had told him that I was making another attempt to quit and he had brought over a medical book with a chapter on smoking. He was a smoker, too, and was trying to be helpful. After he left, I sat down with my cigarettes and the book, and turned to the smoking chapter. At first I found it hard to understand. But I read it again, and something odd started to happen. As I re-read that chapter, a surprising fact emerged.

When nicotine leaves your body you feel empty and insecure. When you smoke another cigarette you put back the nicotine and feel less nervous, or more relaxed, than you did before you lit up.

For the first time I saw that a smoker is like someone who wears tight shoes for the joy of taking them off. Smokers believe that smoking relaxes them and helps them to focus. I believed this, but no longer. Now I understood why I smoked and why every other smoker on the planet smoked. We had all been victims of a massive con: nicotine addiction. The mystery was solved. There and then I decided, 'I'm going to cure the world of smoking.'

I was certain I would never smoke again. I was a non-smoker. I'd escaped. No longer would I feel guilty, weak and ashamed. And I knew that what I had discovered might help others.

When I made the above statement to Joyce, she thought I'd flipped. She had watched so many of my attempts to quit and was bound to have doubts. Also, I hadn't even put out my final cigarette. But from the moment I put together the pieces in my jigsaw, I knew I had found a way to quit that could help other smokers.

Up to that point I had no particular goal in life, other than to live and enjoy each day. Now I had a purpose.

After a few days of freedom from the 'weed', I felt a strong desire to be fit and healthy. Joyce gave me a tracksuit and I took up jogging. I can remember my delight at completing the trip round the block non-stop. About a year later, I ran two half-marathons (more than thirteen miles) in the same week.

When smokers light up they enjoy the relaxed state that was theirs before they started to smoke. They get a taste of what it is like to be a non-smoker. They light a cigarette to get rid of the horrible feeling brought about by the last cigarette. They don't see it like this, of course. They are in the nicotine trap, and brainwashing keeps them smoking.

I had lots of strong arguments against the brainwashing. But I knew that many smokers would need more than that to help them see the truth.

Hypno-therapy can help you relax. I was sure that if smokers were to use my method of quitting, they had to start with an open mind. That was where hypno-therapy would play its part. It would take away any problems crowding the smokers' minds and help them to reach a state in which they were relaxed and able to take in my method.

Joyce was doubtful that I could save the smokers of the world on my own; she was not at all sure that I had saved myself yet. But nothing she or anyone else said could dent my enthusiasm. I was a man with a mission. By this time I was so good at doing up houses that I was working on auto-pilot. While I was earning a living, I was also planning Easyway. I had chosen that name because that was how I had quit – the easy way.

The basis of Easyway is talking with smokers to get rid of their wrong beliefs about cigarettes and why they smoke. Once I had put my arguments into a form I could use, I looked for guinea-pigs. Smokers tend to hang around with other smokers, as I had. Since I had stopped smoking I had become a bit of a bore on the subject, and I talked my friends into letting me try out Easyway on them. Some had no intention of quitting. They didn't mind listening to me talking at them, but they would not join in by either agreeing with what I said or contradicting me.

This taught me an important lesson: the decision to attempt to quit has to be the smoker's. Trying to force someone to take that first step is like putting a man who hates small places into a cupboard. If you get him in, he will try to get out again.

However, other friends wanted to quit. Far from lapping up what I said, they argued with me at every turn. These early sessions were like training for me, and I began to find out what worked and what didn't. It was where I started to hone my method. Even now, more than twenty years on, Easyway is a work in progress, changing and improving to help as many smokers as possible.

After a few weeks I felt ready to take paying customers. Joyce did not want to risk our business, and we decided to look for a place that needed doing up and had space for a clinic. We would run the two businesses side by side until Easyway was doing well. We found a run-down four-bedroom detached house in south-west London that fitted the bill. We planned to convert the lounge into Reception and turn the main bedroom into my clinic.

When I had not smoked for five months, I was ready to send Easyway into the world. The thinking behind Easyway is simple. Instead of focusing on the downsides of smoking – as other methods still do, although all smokers know it's killing them and costing a fortune – Easyway looks at it from the other direction. Why do we smoke in spite of the downsides? With the methods that rely on will-power, smokers have to grit their teeth in the hope that one day they will wake up with no need or wish to smoke. For many, that day never comes. They continue to feel they are missing out and, because of that, they return to smoking or feel unhappy for ever.

Smokers also believe that the unpleasant effects they noticed during failed attempts to stop smoking are caused by lack of nicotine. In fact, you hardly notice the physical withdrawal pangs. The unpleasant feelings are caused by the belief that you are missing out.

Easyway shows the smoker that they have been fooled into thinking they get some sort of pleasure or a crutch from smoking. Soon they understand that this is not so. They stub out their last cigarette, knowing that they will enjoy life more and handle stress better as happy non-smokers. Once smokers understand that they are not giving up anything and that lack of nicotine is not painful, they find there is no need for will-power. Then they find it easy to stop.

I planned to place a small ad in the 'for sale' column of the local paper and go from there. If we had few takers, we'd do up the rest of the house and sell it. Our ad offered as many forty-five-minute sessions as a client needed to quit for a one-off fee of thirty pounds. Most smokers believe that if they can quit for three months, they can quit for ever. If the smokers who came to me smoked again within this period, they would get their money back.

Joyce saw it differently. If most of the people who signed up with me asked for their money back, we would be in trouble. I dug my heels in. In the ad I had claimed a success rate of 75 per cent. If I did not include the guarantee, I might be open to a charge of fraud. I was sure that if I could attract smokers who wanted to quit, I could match the success rate I had claimed. They would see that Easyway was based on honesty.

6 OUR FIRST CLIENT

WE TIMED OUR OPENING to take place at New Year, hoping that we'd get calls from all those people who, as Big Ben struck twelve, had made a resolution to become non-smokers. Indeed calls came, but from friends and family wishing us a happy new year. Over time we learnt that most smokers who make such a resolution break it before they go back to work, or else on the Monday morning of their return.

Joyce and I were like a pair of fathers waiting for the birth of a first child. We were beginning to worry, but then we had a call from a Peter Murray asking about our service. He booked an appointment. I was over the moon to have a client, until Joyce remarked that he had 'sounded like Pete Murray', who was then a celebrity and lived just down the road. For those of you too young to remember him, Pete Murray was a television and radio DJ, who started in the 1950s. We knew his name very well, and I went into a tailspin of fear. However, 'Murray' is quite a common name and the man had called himself 'Peter'.

Joyce and I were watching through the window as Pete Murray strode up our drive. Although I had prepared well, and was pumped up with enthusiasm, the session did not go as I had meant it to. I suppose it would have been the same whoever had been my first client. Before I saw him, my previous sessions had been with people I knew. He could not be expected to make allowances for me and I made none for myself. I couldn't tell what he thought of the session. He remained friendly, even at the end when Joyce had to run round our neighbours to get change for the fifty-pound note he handed over as payment.

From that first session onwards I worked on preparing better arguments to get through to smokers. I had to prove to every one that smoking does not make meals more fun, that it does not relieve stress or boredom, that it does not help you relax or focus. I had to prove that it does the opposite of these things. Also, I had to show them that the cure is not worse than the disease, and you do not have to endure misery while you are trying to quit. Even more important, I had to prove that they wouldn't spend the rest of their lives trying not to smoke.

The Easyway method began as soon as Joyce opened the door to greet a customer. As someone who has always hated the doctor's or dentist's surgery, I wanted our clinic to be friendly and welcoming – a place where people felt able to lower their guard. This was very important for clients who had made several attempts to stop smoking and failed. Many would arrive with a hang-dog look as if they were about to be beaten over the head with another set of demands. I think they were pleasantly surprised to find this was not the case.

We started to make out a history card for each client to help us keep track of their progress. In the first year I was obsessed with measuring our success. At the end of each session I would enter a mark out of 100 for the client. I based it on how well I thought they had understood the method. I was never 100 per cent sure and few scored 90. Those I thought would fail scored 30 and below.

At the end of the first year of Easyway, our success rate – worked out on the money-back guarantee – was 76 per cent. This was more than my wildest dreams. I would have settled for 50 per cent.

The first thank-you letter proved to me that we had at least one satisfied customer. Then we began to get calls from smokers who had heard about my method from others. It was not long before the number of people who joined up by 'word of mouth' was larger than the number who had seen the ad. Our client list was growing weekly, and the sessions now lasted about two hours. At the start, most of our clients were locals but within months smokers were arriving from all over the UK, and then from abroad. One day we had phone calls from smokers who were flying in from South Africa, Italy and the USA!

The ad in the local paper was only bringing in about one client a day, and I was thinking about cancelling it when an article appeared, by the paper's editor, with the headline 'Is he a miracle worker or a charlatan?' If he had looked into Easyway properly, I would have had no quarrel with him, but he hadn't. I cancelled that ad. A few days later, we had a call from the editor to say that the paper's switchboard was being jammed by readers wanting our phone number. Because of this, he was offering to run our ad free of charge. I told him he shouldn't be dealing with a man he thought might be a charlatan – a cheat – let alone passing on his phone number. I no longer wanted an ad in his newspaper, free or not.

Joyce and I could not work out why the ad that had been of little help to us should be of such interest now that it was no longer in the paper. It reminded me of something else I could not explain. Now and again I met a successful client who would tell me that they had recommended Easyway to every smoker they knew, so lots more must be coming to the clinic. I would check our files and see no sign of them.

I decided that even though most smokers want to quit, they put it off till 'tomorrow'. They never do it today. I am sure that many smokers made a mental note of Easyway's name when they saw the ad in the local paper, just as friends of my ex-smoking clients did. When the ad was no longer in the paper, panic set in. If we have a problem to solve, it is important for our peace of mind to know there is a way out. Pretend you are in a room and the door is locked. If you have the key, you won't worry. But if you don't have it, how will you feel?

As a rule, I rang clients a few days after a session to see how they were getting on. Often they would be glad to talk about points they had thought of since our meeting. I would tell them to call me if they wanted to discuss anything else. However, some clients said firmly that they understood the Easyway method very well and that they were fine. I suspected that they were really in need of help and too proud to admit it. But I had to accept what they said and hope I was wrong.

After one such chat, the man's wife called me. She told me that he was nipping outside so often she was sure he was having crafty smokes. Please would I ring him? I didn't want to hassle him, but she begged me to talk to him.

When I rang him, he told me the truth. He had only come to the clinic for his wife's sake. She was the one who wanted him to stop smoking. But some of the things I had said in the session had made him think. Now he didn't know if he wanted to quit or not.

I said: 'First, stop worrying. You will find yourself thinking about smoking. Soon it will become clear to you that you want to be free of it. When that happens, come to see me again.' The next day he rang to fix an appointment. After that session he quit.

Even when a person is committed to stopping smoking, they may need two or more sessions to get into the right frame of mind to do so. They can come to as many sessions as they wish at no extra cost, or phone us, day or night, for support.

Just as I couldn't force smokers into our clinics, I couldn't force them to stay free of smoking. Once they walk out of the clinic they are back in the world where they got hooked on cigarettes. And the hardest time for the ex-smoker comes about six months after his or her session. It seems so long since they smoked that they find it hard to believe they were once a cigarette addict. It is all too easy to say yes to a cigarette, perhaps after a few drinks at a party or when meeting a new friend who smokes. That one cigarette tastes awful. Alarm bells ring. They know they don't want to get hooked again. A few weeks later, they are offered another cigarette. 'I didn't get hooked that last time,' they think, 'so there can't be any harm in having just one now and then.'

In a flash they are back in the trap.

Once I saw a film in which a toad was being eaten legs first by a snake. Eventually, only its head stuck out. It seemed quite happy, as if it had found a warm nest. It didn't seem to know that it was about to die. It is the same with an addict. He or she starts with one cigarette, and is sucked into smoking so slowly that they hardly know what's happening. The very slowness of the process helps them not to think about it. Many smokers will say, 'If it affected my health, I'd give it up,' and then start to cough.

Becoming a smoker is a bit like getting older: the face we see in the mirror today is the same as the one we saw yesterday. But when we look at a photograph taken ten years ago the change is obvious. In the same way, an illness caused by smoking sets in slowly so we tend to ignore it. And when we can't ignore it any longer, we blame it on age rather than smoking.

Some of my clients have had heart surgery. Others have had fingers, toes, arms or legs cut off because they could not stop smoking. Try to imagine your doctor saying, 'Your blood circulation is now so bad that, unless you quit, you are in danger of losing your toes.'

Surely no one would prefer to lose his toes than stop smoking? But the smoker might think the doctor is bluffing to scare him into stopping. He doesn't stop, and he loses his toes.

The doctor now says, 'Unless you stop, you'll lose your feet and perhaps your legs.'

Now the smoker knows the doctor isn't bluffing. Will he go on smoking after this new warning? Many smokers do.

I had no idea how much better my health would be when I stopped smoking until I'd quit. When I smoked I knew I was risking lung cancer, but I blocked my mind to it. I thought I could cope with the other lung problems, the coughing and wheezing. My cough did not worry me, but one of its side-effects did. All the coughing had made a vein in my forehead stick out. One day, I feared, it would burst, and blood would pour out of my mouth, ears, eyes and nose. I blocked this from my mind, as well as the risk of lung cancer.

I thought of lung cancer as hit-or-miss – you were lucky or you weren't. I knew my lungs must be stained with nicotine, but so what? My teeth and fingers were too and it hadn't harmed them. My skin was grey, which I thought was its natural colour. It did not occur to me that it was grey because poison ran in my blood. If I had known that my body had far too little oxygen, and that my immune system was being damaged, I think I would have quit smoking before I found Easyway.

At night when I went to bed, my legs always felt restless. I would ask Joyce to rub them. Soon after I had stopped smoking I no longer needed her to do this.

I had varicose veins, too, before I quit, and sometimes sharp pains in my chest. Both the varicose veins and pain in my chest disappeared when I stopped smoking.

As a child, when I cut myself I was scared by the amount of blood I saw and its bright red colour. Later in life when I cut myself deeply there was hardly any blood, just a browny-red gunge. Now the colour worried me. I knew blood should be bright red. I thought I had a blood disease. When I'd quit I learnt that smoking makes the blood thick and stops oxygen getting to it, so that it turns brown. When I thought of my heart trying to pump that sludge round my body, without missing a beat, I was filled with horror.

When I was in my forties I had liver spots on my hands. Usually, you see them on the hands of the very old. About two years after I had quit, a client told me that when he had stopped smoking, his liver spots had gone. I had forgotten about mine. When I looked for them, they had gone too.

For as long as I can remember, spots had flashed in front of my eyes when I stood up too quickly, often after a hot bath. I felt dizzy and thought I was about to black out. I did not connect this with smoking. I thought it was normal. About two years after I quit, it struck me that it was no longer happening.

Until I stopped smoking I often had a nightmare that I was being chased. I thought this was because my body was missing the nicotine while I slept. After stopping smoking my only nightmare was that I was smoking again.

Ex-smokers often have this dream, and I have been so glad to wake up and realize I am still a non-smoker!

Sometimes, when I was talking about the effect of smoking on us, I would ask: 'Which part of your body has the greatest need of a good supply of blood?'

The grins I got from men told me that they had missed the point. I was talking about the brain! But they were right, too. Many ex-smokers notice that before they quit, their interest in sex has fallen away. They thought this was to do with age. But smoking leads to impotence because of its effect on the blood.

Smokers are fooled into thinking that nicotine helps them: now we can see that it does not. I was shocked when I heard my father say he had no wish to live to be fifty, but twenty years later I felt the same. In the end, because it has made us ill, nicotine even makes us fearful of living.

Any good therapist is able to understand his patients and feel what they feel. I never took people at face value. Each story I heard during the sessions was different and yet the same. As an ex-smoker, I could help people see smoking for what it was without judging them or making them feel a failure. I didn't insult them by telling them what they already knew: that smoking was killing them. Once they understand the nicotine trap, they no longer need to deny the bad side of smoking. The cost to their health and pocket, the slavery, the self-hatred and the anti-social sides of their addiction come to help them score their goal of quitting.

To see smokers arrive in a state of panic, sometimes in tears. To see them sit with their arms folded across their chests, knowing that Easyway has helped other people but sure that it will not be able to help them. To see them unfold their arms, relax and lean forward to take in every word as it dawns on them that they aren't hearing the usual stuff and that Easyway is special. And to watch them leave a little later, already happy non-smokers, some still crying but this time with tears of joy. All of this is rewarding: bringing people to this point and knowing that the process is ongoing with each person. It is also a delight to know how much this help means to the people who receive it.

However, every job has its downside, even

Easyway. For twenty years, clients were allowed to smoke during the session, until they felt the time was right for them to smoke their last cigarette. There are good reasons for this. In fact smoking hinders relaxation and focus, but we cannot explain this to the smoker until later. To ask them not to smoke in the meantime is like asking someone to dive in at the deep end of a pool before they have learnt to swim. Also there are facts about smoking that smokers can only learn before they put out their last cigarette. For example, many smokers believe they enjoy the taste of cigarettes. If you ask them how often they eat a cigarette, they still won't understand that taste has nothing to do with their addiction to smoking.

This policy was the downside. For eight hours a day, often seven days a week, I sat in an atmosphere as polluted as the one I had made before I quit. I might as well have been smoking again for the effect it was having on my breathing. I had avoided lung cancer while I smoked, so the last thing I wanted was to get it through passive smoking. But I was prepared to take the risk. Changing the method was out of the question, because it was so new. Twenty years later we introduced smoking breaks to the sessions without a drop in the success rate. At the time, however, I could not risk that. On fine evenings I would go into the garden, fill my lungs with air and think. I had once polluted my lungs to help me do a job I hated. Now I was polluting my lungs to do a job I loved.

One of the worries of ex-smokers is that a whiff of cigarette smoke will lure them back into the nicotine trap. Indeed, other stop-smoking methods encourage smokers who are attempting to quit not to go into places where cigarettes are smoked. Smokers who had not yet quit often asked me how I managed not to weaken, when I was always near nicotine. Far from making me think I was missing out, the thick air in the clinic confirmed my belief in the evils of smoking. At that time, I was less worried about the unhealthy condition in which I was working, than that I was not keeping pace with the demand for sessions and would not get the word out to enough smokers.

I found a way to improve things when I met a smoker whom I shall call Fred – that's not his real name. Even after more than twenty years of Easyway, I never met a smoker in as bad a state as Fred was, although he had not lost a limb, a lung or had heart surgery. At one time he had been very sporty and fit. Now he looked more dead than alive. He had reached crisis point: that is when a drug addict cannot cope with the amount of the drug he has to take. Fred was using will-power to keep himself down to just five cigarettes a day. He reminded me of myself on that morning when I sat in my car on the brink of making what I now call the Great Escape.

When I met Fred I knew that you cannot quit smoking by cutting down. The longer you go without food, the more hungry you get, until you eat a huge meal. The longer a smoker goes without a cigarette, the more important the cigarette seems when he smokes it.

Fred's nerves were so bad that he couldn't relax enough to listen to what I was saying. He had several sessions, and finally I thought I'd got through to him. The fear left his face, and he smiled, as if the penny had dropped. Then the fear was back. I think Fred slipped through the Easyway net. I never saw or heard of him again.

When I talked about Fred and other sad cases

to friends, they would say things like, 'You can only do your best' or 'Think of all the other lives you've saved.' But I was always left with the thought that if I had done better another smoker might have been saved. I decided that smokers should be able to use Easyway whenever they wanted to, on their own terms.

At the clinics we tell smokers who need more help to ring us at any time, day or night. We also offer extra sessions for free. But some clients don't like to ask for help. That made me think that if I wrote my method down, Fred and smokers like him could read it for themselves until they understood it.

7 GROWING SUCCESS

HOWEVER HARD I WORKED, I could not keep pace with demand. Each happy client would recommend me to their smoking friends, who in turn would recommend me to theirs. I couldn't meet every one of them, but I wanted to let as many people as possible know about Easyway. I telephoned a publisher and explained my method to them. I told them I hadn't yet written the book and would not do so until I had a publisher. I had selected them to be that publisher.

How, I was asked, could they agree to publish a book without first reading it? I said I wasn't writing a novel. My method was tried and tested and would help any smoker to quit for good. The book of the method was bound to be a bestseller.

I was turned down, so I thought about going to another publisher. Then I remembered that

I had read about how difficult it was to get a book published. I decided to pay for 3,000 copies to be printed.

But first I had to write my book. This was in the days before computers and I couldn't type. I needed help, so for six weeks I spent the few hours I had free at the end of each day writing and I passed my hand-written pages to Joyce's daughter, Madeleine, who typed them for me.

Writing *The Easy Way to Stop Smoking* gave me a chance to look into a complaint we were hearing about from some clients. When I quit smoking, the physical pangs of withdrawal from nicotine were so mild I hardly noticed them. But some clients were complaining of pain. Could I really have gone overnight from smoking one hundred cigarettes a day to zero without suffering any pain, or was I so happy to be free that I hadn't noticed it?

The only way to find out the truth was to get hooked again, then quit and look out for pain. When I first discovered Easyway, I didn't understand it, but I knew I was a non-smoker before I put out my final cigarette and would remain one. So when I tried to start smoking again I failed to fall back into the trap. After a month I was up to twenty a day, but it was hard work. I had no wish to smoke. No matter how I tried, I couldn't get hooked again.

For nearly two years I'd been telling clients that one puff on a cigarette could hook them. However, it's not withdrawal from nicotine that hooks a smoker but the idea that they need to smoke. As with any con trick, once you have seen through it you won't fall for it again. If you are a non-smoker or an ex-smoker, please don't test this. You have nothing to gain and much to lose. But you can try this: dig your nails into an arm or leg. Although you will hurt yourself, you won't be stressed by it. This is because you are in control. You know the cause of the pain and can stop it when you choose. Now, if the same level of pain was to occur in your head or chest without you knowing why, you would soon be very stressed.

A smoker believes that the pain he or she suffers when they stop smoking is due to lack of nicotine. In fact, it is in the mind. They want a cigarette because they think they will enjoy it or it will give them a crutch. Once they see that cigarettes are the cause of stress, not a cure for it, they can no more believe in their need to smoke than they can kid themselves the earth is flat. It was a key point that I made in my book.

When our 3,000 copies of *The Easy Way to Stop Smoking* arrived, we were so busy running the clinic that we had no time to sell it, other than putting the book in the waiting room. After a year, we'd sold about a hundred copies. I suppose that showed how successful the sessions were. Once clients saw themselves as non-smokers, they had no need to buy a book about the method.

One of the first celebrities to book an Easyway session was the actor Patrick Cargill. A few weeks later, during an interview for a local radio station in Brighton, he talked about his session and how taken he was with the method. Soon afterwards the producer of that show invited me for an interview. I thought this would be a good opportunity to unload some copies of the book and asked an old friend, a first-rate salesman, to go to the biggest bookshop in Brighton. They agreed to take some copies. A girl called Sharon, who had tried everything to quit, heard my interview and bought a copy. She read it, and sent a copy to

Derek Jameson. He had edited several of the UK's leading tabloid papers, and had then moved to radio and television broadcasting. His no-nonsense, down-to-earth approach to life had won a large audience for his Radio 2 breakfast show.

One morning shortly before Christmas 1984 Joyce took a call from one of his team. We were told that Derek had made several attempts to quit smoking but with little success, until he had received that copy of *Easy Way*. He had read it some six weeks ago and hadn't smoked since. Would I be interviewed on his programme? I was delighted. I saw a chance for Easyway to become better known.

I went into the studio, nerves jangling at the prospect of giving a live interview. You can imagine my surprise when Derek waded in with: 'I hate you, I hate you! This man has forced me to give up smoking.'

I could have throttled him. In my quest to rid the world of smoking, this was my first break-through. I had the chance to tell four million people that the methods smokers normally use to quit make it harder for them to do so. Now Derek Jameson, who was grateful to Easyway, had undermined my method in his first words.

I spent the rest of the interview trying to reverse the spin Derek had put on the method, but I feared the damage had been done. At the end he signed off with a cheery plug: 'I'm not supposed to advertise, but it's a good cause. Send a five-pound cheque or postal order and you'll have a copy of the book by return of post.'

All credit to him for ignoring the BBC's strict no-advertising rule. I was disappointed with the interview, but the prospect of getting rid of a few copies of *Easy Way* made me feel a bit better.

On the morning after the show, we waited for the postman. He walked past our gate. There was no post for us. At about eleven o'clock the front-door bell rang. Outside was a bright red post-office van, and on our doorstep three fat mailbags.

Joyce and I could not have been more excited if I had met her perfectly timed cross to head in England's winning goal against Brazil in a World Cup final. We had blown £3,000 on printing a book that had sold barely 100 copies in a year. Then, out of the blue, £25,000 worth of orders landed on our doorstep in a single day – and again on the next three days. Between orders we found the odd Christmas card. I joked to Joyce: 'Tell our friends to enclose a fiver!'

It seemed that Derek had hit just the right spot when he said: 'This man has forced me to give up smoking.' Isn't that what all smokers are looking for – a method that will force them to stop, whether they like it or not? The thousands of letters we received agreed with Derek Jameson.

That interview had two important results. A senior editor at Penguin Books heard it and asked me to send her a few copies. She handed them out to members of her staff who wanted to quit smoking. Their success led her to take over the book. *The Easy Way to Stop Smoking* first appeared in Penguin in 1985. Since then it has become a world bestseller and has sold more than seven million copies.

The second effect of the interview was a mixed blessing. We took a huge number of bookings. I was already working flat out and couldn't keep up with demand. I had no choice but to look at holding group sessions.

We decided to set an upper limit of eleven for each one. The individual sessions had started at about forty-five minutes, and became longer as I improved the method and added new arguments to make the difference between success and failure. I brought the same thinking to the group sessions. At the outset these lasted about two hours, and are now five hours long.

I worried that with eleven people my success rate might be lower. To my relief, this turned out not to be the case. It continued to rise.

When we started to think about expanding, Joyce and I decided that our second clinic should be in Birmingham. It was soon up and running, and within six months was paying its way.

It has been said to me that Easyway's growth must have been greatly helped by the many well-known people who have sought my help. Marti Caine, Patrick Cargill, Johnny Cash, Christopher Cazenove, Julie Christie, Fish, Frederick Forsyth, Emma Freud, Leslie Grantham, Robin Jackman, Matthew Kelly, Mark Knopfler, Rula Lenska, Ian Maxwell, John Cougar Mellencamp, Jenni Murray, John Sessions, Nina Simone, Dennis Waterman,

Ruby Wax and Susannah York, to name but a few. I am lucky to count Sir Richard Branson and Sir Anthony Hopkins as two of my most out-spoken supporters.

Everyone comes to Easyway for the same reason. If you are a smoker, sooner or later you will want to escape from the trap. I have helped to expand the initial success of the method and reach a much wider audience. I am lucky to have had the help of so many clever and hard-working people, and I am proud of what we have done to date.

8 EXPANSION OVERSEAS

Smokers travel from all over the world to visit my Easyway clinics. In the early days I found that smokers from countries in the north were more successful than those from the south. The Germans and Dutch did well, the French, Italians and Spanish less so. At Easyway we agreed that people were more relaxed about smoking in the south than they were in the north, so people in the south saw less need to quit. Also, clients from the north often spoke English better than those from the south.

When we looked at the success rates of English people against those from abroad, we found that even those from overseas who spoke good English failed to understand the Easyway message. It is easy to miss a point in a language that is not your own, and English is complex. I was not surprised that some of our non-British clients struggled. I gave them as much help as I could, but I could not make up for their problems with the English language. Many had come a very long way to attend a session, and I felt bad when they left without having understood properly what we were trying to tell them. Some must have felt that their last chance of escape had gone.

It has always been Easyway's aim to reach every smoker, wherever they are, so that they can use my method to quit. When Easyway had just started, I had letters from ex-clients wishing to become therapists, some of whom lived abroad. A young woman called Eveline wanted to set up a clinic in Holland. I thought Easyway might not help in countries where English is not the first language. However, Eveline's clinic was a success, and when she had translated my first book into Dutch it became a bestseller in Holland. That was when I knew that the Easyway method could work across the world – as long as those who present it understand it and can express it correctly in their own language.

By 2003 we had nineteen clinics outside the UK. In places where smoking has been thought the norm, I had been concerned about Easyway's chances of success, but even in Spain, Italy, Portugal and South America Easyway is as successful as anywhere else.

Easyway is growing because committed people are taking it forward. For Easyway's method to work, it has to be presented by people who believe in, and understand, it and the thinking that lies behind it. This is rare in a world where how much you sell is more important than what you sell. Because the Easyway therapists share common aims and values, they are close-knit even though they are separated by huge distances.

Easyway has also grown because clients recommend it to others. However, in recent years many people have come to us when their workplace has become non-smoking. In the early days I had a lovely surprise when a string of people turned up from the same company. I am doing something right, I thought.

Everyone comes to Easyway to quit smoking, even those who might seem to be on the other side of the fence. When the director of a big tobacco company arrived at the clinic, I was suspicious. Why would he want a session? It turned out that he was the only member of his board who still smoked, and the others wanted him to stop. Other people from the firm started to book sessions too. Like any other group of smokers, these people wanted to be free. I suppose it makes sense. If you are a smoker, you will want to escape from the trap, even if you make your living selling cigarettes.

With the ranks of non-smokers swelling fast, bosses are now looking to solve the problems that arise with smokers in a work force. A smoker spends about 115 hours per year on cigarette breaks, and takes at least five days more sick leave per year than a non-smoker. Also, there is often a gulf between smokers and non-smokers at work. Non-smokers resent the extra breaks that the smokers can take. Many companies ask us to help cure their work force of smoking. We run sessions for them at our clinics, at their offices or somewhere else of their choosing. Sir Richard Branson was one of the first businessmen to contact Easyway for his staff. He was convinced that the method worked.

In the last few years Easyway has helped BMW, BP, British Airways, DHL, Ford, Guinness, Hilton Hotels, IBM, IKEA, the Inland Revenue, Marks & Spencer, Microsoft, Nestlé, O2, Schweppes, Sony, Woolworths and other large companies.

This list is still growing. The world of business has taken to Easyway because the method has worked for many people and will continue to do so.

At the end of *The Easy Way to Stop Smoking*, I wrote: 'There is a wind of change in society. A snowball has started that I hope this book will turn into an avalanche.'

The twentieth anniversary of my discovery of Easyway fell on 15 July 2003. I think that by now the snowball is the size of a football. I am proud of Easyway's success and of all the effort that many committed people have put into it.

Although I haven't seen the avalanche, Easyway's supporters will. The truth about quitting smoking will come out, and will not be silenced. Only in the last five hundred years has it been agreed that the Earth is round, not flat. Experts have always got facts wrong, but once a course is set it takes time to change ideas. Wrong thinking becomes stuck in minds closed to change.

In the not too distant future, smoking will be something we used to do. And I am sure that Easyway will have played a large part in bringing this about. As often happens, people will find their own salvation where smoking is concerned – and many will choose Easyway to help them.

My stop-smoking books will, I am sure, make the decision easier and that football-sized snowball will go on getting bigger. During the summer of 2006 I was told I had lung cancer and that an operation wouldn't help.* Those smoky sessions might or might not have caused it, but that doesn't matter to me. I have had twenty-three years of happy, healthy life and that would not have been the case if I hadn't stopped when I did. I have been the happiest man in the world. I have cured around ten million smokers across the world, and it is a price worth paying.

* See Publisher's Note on p. xi.

EPILOGUE

WATCHING SOMEONE CHANGE FROM smoker to non-smoker is, for me, about as good as life gets. There is a saying about being a victim of one's own success. In one sense that happened to me with Easyway's growth. It meant I could no longer spend 99 per cent of my time working with clients. Instead I had to write books, give interviews and keep in touch with problem smokers.

I don't feel comfortable with the public side of success, being interviewed, travelling or staying in hotels. And I hate being photographed. All in all, I am the world's most reluctant front man. But I don't complain about it. It's all part of a debt of gratitude I can never repay.

Because of Easyway, I was released from accountancy and nicotine addiction. Without it I would not have enjoyed the happiness and excitement of the last twenty-three years.

I would have looked back on my life as a gift wasted.

I have seen my method published in books in more than forty countries. Last year we made a DVD version of the method, recorded in English, German, Spanish and French, and it is being dubbed and sub-titled in many other languages. Allen Carr's Easyway will continue its work long after my time has passed, and Robin Hayley, who has been my friend for more than fifteen years, will go on expanding Easyway as he has done for the past decade.

I think of myself as luckier than any man has a right to be. Luck is available to everyone and I am a true believer in it. I only began to take it seriously after that turning point twenty-three years ago. With Joyce, it has been my constant companion ever since. Work with it and you, too, will find it generous.

TELL ALLEN CARR'S EASYWAY ORGANIZATION THAT YOU HAVE STOPPED SMOKING!

Leave a comment on www.allencarr.com, email yippee@allencarr.com or write to the Worldwide Head Office address shown below.

ALLEN CARR'S EASYWAY CLINICS

The following list indicates the countries where Allen Carr's Easyway To Stop Smoking Clinics are currently operational. The success rate at the clinics, based on the money-back guarantee, is over 90 per cent.

Allen Carr guarantees you will find it easy to stop smoking at his clinics or your money back. Selected clinics also offer sessions that deal with alcohol and weight issues. Please check with your nearest clinic for details.

ALLEN CARR'S EASYWAY
Worldwide Head Office
Park House, 14 Pepys Road, Raynes Park,
London SW20 8NH, ENGLAND
Tel: +44 (0)208 9447761
Email: mail@allencarr.com
Website: www.allencarr.com

Worldwide Press Office
Tel: +44 (0)7970 88 44 52
Email: jd@statacom.net

UK Clinic Information and Central Booking Line
Tel: 0800 389 2115 (Freephone)

UNITED KINGDOM	ITALY
REPUBLIC OF IRELAND	JAPAN
AUSTRALIA	MAURITIUS
AUSTRIA	MEXICO
BELGIUM	NETHERLANDS
CANADA	NEW ZEALAND
CARIBBEAN	NORWAY
(GUADELOUPE,	POLAND
ANTILLES)	PORTUGAL
COLOMBIA,	SERBIA
SOUTH AMERICA	SLOVAKIA
CZECH REPUBLIC	SOUTH AFRICA
DENMARK	SPAIN
ECUADOR,	SWEDEN
SOUTH AMERICA	SWITZERLAND
FRANCE	TURKEY
GERMANY	USA
GREECE	
ICELAND	

Visit www.allencarr.com to access your
nearest clinic's contact details.

READ ON THE BEACH!
Win a holiday to Barbados

Fly to the beautiful four-star **Amaryllis Beach Resort** set on a white, sandy beach on the south coast of Barbados.

For more information about the resort please visit www.amaryllisbeachresort.com. letsgo2.com

Other prizes to be won
- **£100-worth of books for all the family**
  (we have five sets to give away)

- **A limousine for an evening in London**

- **£100-worth of M&S vouchers**
  (we have two sets to give away)

HOW TO ENTER
Fill in the form below.
Name two authors who have written Quick Reads books:

1. _____

2. _____

Your name: _____

Address: _____

_____

Telephone number: _____

Tell us where you heard about Quick Reads: _____

_____

☐ **I have read and agree to the terms and conditions on the back of this page**

Send this form to: Quick Reads Competition, Colman Getty, 28 Windmill Street, London, W1T 2JJ or enter the competition on our website www.quickreads.org.uk.
Closing date: 1 September 2007

QUICK READS COMPETITION

TERMS AND CONDITIONS

1. You must be aged 18 years or older and resident in the UK to enter this competition. If you or an immediate family member works or is otherwise involved in the Quick Reads initiative or in this promotion, you may not enter.

2. To enter, fill in the entry form in the back of a Quick Reads book, in ink or ballpoint pen, tear it out and send it to: Quick Reads Competition, Colman Getty, 28 Windmill Street, London W1T 2JJ before the closing date of 1 September 2007. Or enter on our website at www.quickreads.org.uk before 1 September 2007.

3. You may enter as many times as you wish. Each entry must be on a separate form found in the back of a Quick Reads book or a separate entry on the www.quickreads.org.uk website. No entries will be returned.

4. By entering this competition you agree to the terms and conditions.

5. We cannot be responsible for entry forms lost, delayed or damaged in the post. Proof of posting is not accepted as proof of delivery.

6. The prizes will be awarded to the people who have answered the competition questions correctly and whose entry forms are drawn out first, randomly, by an independent judge after the closing date. We will contact the winners by telephone by 1 November 2007.

7. There are several prizes:
   First Prize (there will be one first prize-winner) – Seven nights' stay at a four-star resort in Barbados. The holiday is based on two people sharing a self-catering studio room with double or twin beds and includes: return flights from a London airport, seven nights' accommodation (excludes meals), use of the resort gym and non-motorised water sports. Travel to and from the London airport is not included. You will be responsible for airport transfers, visa, passport and insurance requirements, vaccinations (if applicable), passenger taxes, charges, fees and surcharges (the amount of which is subject to change). You must travel before 1 May 2008. You must book at least four weeks before departure and bookings will be strictly subject to availability. The prize-winner will be bound by the conditions of booking issued by the operator.
   Second Prize (there will be five second prize-winners) – A set of books selected by the competition Promoter including books suitable for men, women and children – to be provided by Quick Reads up to the retail value of £100.
   Third Prize (there will be one third prize-winner) – An evening in a limousine travelling around London between the hours of 6 p.m. and midnight in a limousine provided by us. You and up to five other people will be collected from any one central London point and can travel anywhere within inner London. Champagne is included. Travel to and from London is not included.
   Fourth Prize (there will be two fourth prize-winners) – £100-worth of Marks & Spencer vouchers to be spent in any branch of M&S.

8. There is no cash alternative for any of these prizes and unless agreed otherwise in writing the prizes are non-refundable and non-transferable.

9. The Promoter reserves the right to vary, amend, suspend or withdraw any or all of the prizes if this becomes necessary for reasons beyond its control.

10. The names and photographs of prize-winners may be used for publicity by the Promoter, provided they agree at the time.

11. Details of prize-winners' names and counties will be available for one month after the close of the promotion by writing to the Promoter at the address set out below.

12. The Promoter, its associated companies and agents, exclude responsibility for any act or failure by any third-party supplier, including airlines, hotels or travel companies, as long as this is within the law. Therefore this does not apply to personal injury or negligence.

13. The Promoter is Quick Reads/World Book Day Limited, 272 Vauxhall Bridge Road, London SW1V 1BA.

Quick Reads
Pick up a book today

Quick Reads are published alongside and in partnership with BBC RaW.

We would like to thank all our partners in the Quick Reads project for their help and support:

NIACE
unionlearn
National Book Tokens
The Vital Link
The Reading Agency
National Literacy Trust
Booktrust
Welsh Books Council
The Basic Skills Agency, Wales
Accent Press
Communities Scotland

Quick Reads would also like to thank the Department for Education and Skills, Arts Council England and World Book Day for their sponsorship, and NIACE (the National Institute for Adult Continuing Education) for their outreach work.

Quick Reads is a World Book Day initiative.

Quick Reads

Books in the Quick Reads series

New titles

A Dream Come True	Maureen Lee
Burning Ambition	Allen Carr
Lily	Adèle Geras
Made of Steel	Terrance Dicks
Reading My Arse	Ricky Tomlinson
The Sun Book of Short Stories	
Survive the Worst and Aim for the Best	Kerry Katona
Twenty Tales from the War Zone	John Simpson

Backlist

Blackwater	Conn Iggulden
Book Boy	Joanna Trollope
Chickenfeed	Minette Walters
Cleanskin	Val McDermid
Danny Wallace and the Centre of the Universe	Danny Wallace
Don't Make Me Laugh	Patrick Augustus
The Grey Man	Andy McNab
Hell Island	Matthew Reilly
How to Change Your Life in Seven Steps	John Bird
I Am a Dalek	Gareth Roberts
The Name You Once Gave Me	Mike Phillips
Star Sullivan	Maeve Binchy

Don't get by ~~get on~~ 0800 100 900

We provide courses for anyone who wants to develop their skills. All courses are free and are available in your local area. If you'd like to find out more, phone 0800 100 900.

First Choice Books

If you enjoyed this Quick Reads book, you'll find more great reads on www.firstchoicebooks.org.uk or at your local library.

First Choice is part of The Vital Link, promoting reading for pleasure. To find out more about The Vital Link visit www.vitallink.org.uk.

Find out what the BBC's RaW (Reading and Writing Campaign) has to offer at www.bbc.co.uk/raw.

Quick Reads

Twenty Tales from Tales from the War Zone
by John Simpson

Pan Books

As a top television journalist, John Simpson has been involved in many dangerous and hair-raising events. *Twenty Tales from the War Zone* brings together the most powerful, shocking and, also, hilarious experiences of his career. It includes amazing stories from the many wars he has covered, from Northern Ireland to Iraq, from Kosovo to Kabul.

Whether crossing the border into Afghanistan disguised as a woman or being kidnapped at gunpoint in the back streets of Belfast, Simpson paints a vivid picture of what being a journalist on the front line is all about. It's a rollercoaster ride that is sure to thrill anyone who dares to join it.

'A first-rate writer and funny with it' John Humphreys, *Sunday Telegraph*

Quick Reads

Reading My Arse!
by Ricky Tomlinson

Sphere

Hot on the heels of bestsellers *Football My Arse!* and *Celebrities My Arse!*, from the ever-popular master storyteller Ricky Tomlinson, comes a funny and maverick novel about one man's decision to explore the world and how reading helps him on his quest.

L i v e   m o r e

If you would like to receive more information on Healthy
Penguin titles, authors, special offers, events and giveaways,
please email HealthyPenguin@uk.penguingroup.com